Lower-Class Heresy

Lower-Class Heresy

POEMS BY

T. R. Hummer

University of Illinois Press   *Urbana and Chicago*

Publication of this work was supported in part by grants from the National Endowment for the Arts and the Illinois Arts Council, a state agency.

This book is printed on acid-free paper.

Some of the poems have previously appeared in the following journals, and are reprinted by permission:

Bennington Review: Inner Ear
Chariton Review: Voice and Room, in the Course of Time
Crazyhorse: Sister of Mercy Charity Ward, Lights Out; Northeast, a Bend in the River
Georgia Review: The Second Story; The Immoralities: Drunk All Afternoon
Hudson Review: Legal Limit; The Underworld
Kenyon Review: Winter, a Walk in Pinewoods; Cancer Rising; The Ideal; The Real; Dogma: Pigmeat and Whiskey
Missouri Review: In Far Light, the Kinship of Sisters
New Virginia Review: Convention: An Alternative; The Unpoetic; Well-Being; The Lost
New Yorker: The Future
Quarterly West: The Cold
Tendril: A Clearing in Pennsylvania; In Shock
Slackwater Review: From Overland, a Postcard; The Afterworld
Western Humanities Review: An Abandoned Farm in the West

"The Sun" and "Empty Backstreet in a Small Southern Town" first appeared in *New American Poets of the 1980's*, ed. Myers and Weingarten, Wampeter Press, 1985.

for Theo

CONTENTS

I

The Subscendentalists

*I stand in awe of my body, this matter to which
I am bound has become so strange to me. I fear not
spirits, ghosts of which I am one . . . but I fear bodies,
I tremble to meet them. What is this Titan that has
possession of me? Talk of mysteries!*

—THOREAU

INNER EAR

Think of it this way, the doctor tells him,
A small sealed chamber with a fine dust inside.
He thinks of a country church, that tiny unused room
Where they keep old choir robes nobody ever wears.
He went there once with the girl who made a mistake

In Sunday school. "'Consider,'" she read aloud,
"'The lilies of the field. They do not sow,
Neither do they rape.'" The red she turned
When everybody laughed was a miracle.

The dust is always settling, always falling.
Your body knows. That's how it tells up from down.
Lying flat on his back in a hospital bed
He thinks it incredibly strange
That the spinning he feels in the world is not in the world

But in the dust inside his head.
It is true that the world is turning,
And its motionlessness is only apparent.
It is not true he feels it turning,

But maybe a doubling of illusions
Amounts to something like the truth.
That small room at the back of the church has a window in it.
When she grabs his hand and pulls him in,
They stand together in its hot shaft of light.

Have you ever kissed a girl, she whispers.
He doesn't answer, he just kisses her.
Sometimes it can be like that. It hits him
While he is driving. One minute everything is fine,

The next, everything turns upside down.
The nausea is indescribable. He goes so gray
His wife is certain it is his heart.
He sits there while she flags a passing car, his eyes shut,
His forehead jammed on top of the steering wheel

3

Which gives him no clues, being round.
In the hospital bed he lies carefully, not moving his head.
Everything that falls, he thinks, *falls*
Toward the center of some larger body.

Dust falls toward the center of the earth.
The girl is older than he is, almost sixteen.
She has to bend to kiss him.
He keeps his eyes open, sees how tight hers clench.
Her tongue darts in his mouth. She holds him hard.

Dust motes rise around them in the sunlight,
Shimmering in a translucent eddy as if their bodies
Were an obstacle in some current.
Sometimes, the doctor says, *there'll be a disturbance.*

We don't know why it happens. But when it does,
The dust can't settle. And then your sense of direction
Goes haywire. You don't know which way is up.
His wife sits by the bed reading an article aloud:
I Am Joe's Inner Ear. "The inner ear as a whole

Is referred to as *the labyrinth.* There are, in fact,
Two labyrinths, one inside the other."
"It's a hell of a clumsy way to do things,"
He says. "It's a crude piece of engineering."

"I thought it was your heart," she says. "I knew it was."
He stares at the ceiling, not turning to look at her.
"There's no connection," he says, "between the heart
And the inner ear." But he lies there holding on
To the bedrail's steel, believing he can feel

The pole tilt toward the solstice.
Bony labyrinth, he hears his wife murmur, *membranous labyrinth.*
An out-of-tune pedal organ in a distant room wheezes out
Rock of ages, cleft for me.

Listen, the girl whispers, *listen,*
But he stands straight and kisses her again and again.
There is only the rush of blood in his ears
And the voice that tells him *Really, we don't know much.*
It could happen any time. It may never happen again.

LEGAL LIMIT

an adulterers' story

No matter what it means
To jerk one up
Through scum-green

Surface, out of the depth
Of murk lake water is,
I landed it, a bream

Too small to keep. But I was
So young it seemed
Huge, big as both

The hands you hold against you
In your half-
Sleep, my hands, grown now

Out of that boy's measure
Into yours: a man's,
Ready for the obscure

Shapes a woman's skin
Takes in dark rooms, ready
To quicken to your childlike mumble

When you say *Tell me a story.*
Touching you, I can tell
How my hands in memory are

Strangely diminished, as though
I am not seeing them as they were
But focus the boy I was through

The backward-distancing lens
This story can't help being:
The dangled fish, the hands,

The boy and his unknowing
Of what is and is not enough.
I kept it, I looped a string

In a slipknot through the sawtooth
Bloodred of gills, swung
That blade-thin bright body back

Against algaed surface tension
Right-angled into the soup of lake,
The willow limb I tied it on

Unnaturally quivering in the darkening
Evening. I walked away down the dam,
Still hungry for that quickening

Rod in my hands. And now I am
Cupping the curious weight
Of your breasts as you turn

To listen, I am wishing I could say
I went back in that blind afternoon
And missed it, but the truth is

I clean forgot about it,
That goddamned little fish
I guess I knew in my heart

Was not worth fooling with:
Diminished in memory, in story, to
A trembling, a breath

Of wind on water where there is no
Wind, a ripple at midnight,
A rising. And when I come

Again months later, I remember it
Only when I stumble
Over a limp length

Of string. I pull on it:
In that moment of resistance, I clench
Both hands hard, drag it out:

Lying above you now,
The story almost over,
I see it again, I know

What surfaces obscure,
What strikes from below
In starved, bone-jarring motion:

The snake and the small fish it swallowed
Both caught on that twine and torn clean
By quick-kissing mouths to

An intricate fusion of skeleton
No skill of hands can undo:
These two made one.

Dark, this room could be anywhere, could be
Any time, could be the room
Of my childhood, or of two nights ago
When a woman lay in the dark beside me

Hearing the watch by the bed speak time
And time's syllables, sentences.
If I touch her, I can feel
That voice in the gather of her breast

As the knot of her nipple tenses
Her breath in my palm. It is still
Here without her, and I
Laugh at myself, the cliché

It tells me my life is, a song on the radio,
Bad soap opera, a story
You can hear any day
In any bar in town. To the east,

Mountains clot under starlight, but my one
Window faces west. It is blank, a patch
Of dark two shades grayer than the rest
Of what must be wall: no shape, no direction

To this room tonight but what I give it,
So I make it big, make it open
On pastureland in June starlight,
Fog smeared glowing in the slit

Between black leaf-mass of hedgerow and ground.
I am walking hip-pocket high
To my father, who does not speak
But whistles one long note

At the bird dog rustling invisibly
In Johnson grass. I see my father take
Something from the khaki
Pocket over his heart,

A cigarette suddenly white
Against the colorlessness of body
Under stars: I see him start
To say something, hear

The breath about to be words whistle in
The pit of his nostrils, see his mouth
Open on dark where
The voice will come from when

It comes: *now,* I think, *now:*
But his mouth is shapeless,
Huge: inside it the window shimmers,
Its stars obscured by the city's gray glow,

And when she comes to me, wordless
And blind from the flat glare
Of the hall light, backlit
In the doorframe, face deep in shadow,

I reach, and my hands go through her
Incandescent refraction of hair,
Search her face, find her mouth, cover it,
The name it is starting to whisper,

The voice that is starting to whisper it.

FROM OVERLAND, A POSTCARD

Nothing can tell me what is coming, love, not the lights
Of Joplin, Missouri at two A.M., or the sign
I wake to, hung just out the bus window, hand-shaped:

Madame Rose, Palmist, Psychic, Healer.
A woman. A long journey. Love. Say it:
Who is this man come to be

Touched and known, dead of a summer evening?
Through two tinted layers of glass and twenty yards
Of scorched Missouri air, I make them out:

A preacherly young man, a woman with a goiter.
In the hard white light of that parlor
They have opaque faces. The young man's hands

Are outstretched, his head tilts
Sideways. He is listening, waiting.
The woman stares at him. She does not speak.

The space between them blurs in my mirrored face.
Inside the bus, a pale green light
Comes from nowhere, the travelers' bodies

Glow green in sleep. I cannot see
What they look like, only the radioactive shining
Of their flesh. We have come together

A long way: Pittsburgh, Columbus, St. Louis,
Two days west of you in a bus called *Tulsa Express.*
We do not know each others' names. But now, awake

In a place I have never been, I can tell you
Stories: the small slumped aura
Of the boy across the aisle is marked:

He will love hopelessly, travel great distances.
In the clenched hands of the dreaming man beside him
I read passion, a woman's face, a sin so great

There is nothing left to do but ride it out.

11

A CLEARING IN PENNSYLVANIA

Against the sudden needled rise
Of trees on a steep hillside,
It opens its still, level cove
Of grass and wildflowers nameless

To the uninitiated.
But nobody comes here to name things.
This is nowhere on a back road
Between somewhere and somewhere in Pennsylvania.

I brake my car on the shoulder,
Step out, step off the cinders,
Take three paces and stand
At the center of this clearing,

This place nobody thinks of,
Where for who knows what reason trees
Stop growing down the rocky hillface
And only their shadows come forward.

It is small. It is insignificant.
I could say it is like the space
Lovers make for themselves
In the middle of other lives,

But no one could hear me, or know
The irony I use against my own
Simile's desperate rhetoric.
There is only one question worth asking: why

Have I stopped here?
On some other road beyond
This hill, a motorcycle's engine
Backfires, dopplers, downshifts, each

Cylinder-prick of its passing
A metallic beating in my spine.
Wherever it goes, something human
Hangs on. It is easy here to imagine

That silence is natural wisdom,
But silence is death. Put a house
With boarded-up windows here,
Brace it hard against the hillside,

Hang abandoned barn swallows' nests
In its eaves, give it untended flowers
With names: delphinium gone to seed.
It will be, at odd moments

When accident brings someone
To stand here, silent
As any clichéd grave.
This clearing has a natural purpose

Stark as Darwin's explanation
For the miraculous coloration of moths.
Who knows what it is? Who cares?
This place is part of a place

With a human name. That's why I say
Pennsylvania, a nonsense sound
Which locates me.
And I could come here again

With a woman, to touch her
On this grass, to make
Those sounds the touch of the human
Gives us, against nature, whenever it comes

In the red shift of the heart:
That's why I say *a clearing in.*

IN FAR LIGHT, THE KINSHIP OF SISTERS

Odor of strange food, pale
Northern beans: odor
Of starch, of stale

Standing air:
Recoil of home-brewed
Permanents, honey-dull hair

Washed and screwed
Into meat-pink
Curlers: residue

In that house of caustic
Detergents, blueing, bleach,
Burnt-flesh scorch-stink

Of ironing: and bodies, each
Scrubbed clean, but all together
Breathing that alien breath

Of otherness. She is there,
My aunt, one body among them,
Bleeding her fair share

Of distance into this room
Where I sit shy
Beside my mother. We have come

Driving days through the rolling infinity
Of the Midwest, out of the resinous
Air of Pine-Belt Mississippi,

Through Arkansas, Oklahoma, Kansas,
My mother wrestling the old black Ford,
I in the back seat, half comatose

With grit from the wind-scarred
Prairie, with July heat,
With miles: six years old and scared

That whirl of dust and wheat
Will let us fall so hard
Into its harsh-slanted light

We will forget how far
Away from everything
We know we really are:

Run miles from my father to this wrong-
Smelling house in deep Nebraska,
This family of odd-spoken

Kin: drunk uncle with nothing to say,
Ratchet-voiced girl cousins
With one face, hair the raw color of whiskey,

And she, with her soap-rasped hands
On my cheeks, turning my head
To profile, galling the skin.

Why, she says to my mother, *he's you, I'd
Know him anywhere.*
I twist in her grip, slide

Off the sofa, face her,
This woman I have never seen,
My mother's sister:

See on her my mother's face, gone
Oddly drawn, older,
Pinched, foreign,

But unmistakably there.
Smoke of bacon grease, incense
Of mothballs and ammonia in that air,

Odor of sweatsoaked elastic, dense
Aura of onions, chewing gum, lye:
Smell in that house a senseless

Dizziness as she leans to kiss me. She
Is my mother's face, she is mine. The room
Fills with the stale intensity

Of dime-store perfume,
Her lips touch a cheek, and I see the mirror-
Eyes of her unnameable daughters come

To focus on me together,
Anonymous, all of us, whoever
Any of us are:

And I hear someone whisper
To someone behind me *You see? There's
Nothing in him of his father:*

He's no more that man than you are.

SISTERS: A FAMILY CHRONICLE

i. *Winter: A Walk in Pinewoods*

Sometime, but not too long from now, it will come to you
That nothing you hear in the trees is trying to speak.
You have listened all this time without questioning
Even for a second where it comes from, but the moment
Is not far off when you will hear that voice you believe in break

Like a pubescent boy's, and you will never again even think
In the language you thought you heard
Saying, over and over, something you understood:
These are the woods, those are the clouds, this is the cold echo
Of wind that moves between. Today I am here, I tell you, and you

God help you, are my sister: but these are words, and only
Keep you from knowing the prickling
Voice you will hear soon enough and believe is breaking
Now, in its time, out of that other cold
Certainty, out of that needled questioning of your body.

ii. *The Long Pier*

What you call in memory *stain*
Is nothing, is the shadow
On a gray-weathered cypress pier
Of willow driven dense by summer,
Or wind-stippled lake water's color
Deepened by July afternoon.
You are outside it. In the blaze
Of that season, I see
How you lie, thirteen again,
The white of your T-shirt lifted
By the swell of what I cannot have
Called *breasts*. I know how it darkens
In your mind to rust
Or the brown of dried blood,
Tintype sepia. But that
Is wrong. It is clear. You believe
No one will ever see you
Touched that way by your skin's
Translation of sun. But I stare
As you uncross your arms,
Lift that translucence
Of shirt, your eyes
Closed in what I know
Is blinding, both of us
Uncertain I will not come
Out of willow-shade that holds me
Invisible, to lie
Beside you, touch that strange
Flesh-dark aureole you feel now
Through no distance of memory still
Burned in that light, and your own.

iii. *Sister of Mercy Charity Ward, Lights Out*

I should recognize it, night
Or alley-shadow or the quick sleep
That comes from a beer bottle swung
Sudden against my temple—

One way or the other, dark
I should have expected, but forgot
Until it was almost too late.
But in what gathers there is still

The other thing, the white sweep
Of the woman's dress as she goes
Out through the fading rectangle
Of door. She is quiet as she humanly can be

But still she raises a vanishing latch-rattle,
The quick silver squeal of a hinge,
And I turn to see it coming just in time
To think her face is the same as the face

I touched in the near-instantaneous pain
Of love. It is somewhere in time,
The other man's name she was, the good
Salt-taste of skin between her breasts,

But there *is* no time. I might be
Any age, any face, my hand the hand of a stranger:
This much mercy can dance
On the hollow tip of a needle.

And I know what it was, your coming
Sudden in the sudden dark beside me,
Mouth open, the word you spoke
As the cold in the vein of my arm

Turns to touch me kindly.

iv. *Northeast: A Bend in the River*

Here you can go right down to the water.
It is easy. You do not even have to climb,
And nothing will punish you. You are grown now,
A woman. It is yours to choose. You choose,

And you are here. Far out over the glycerin
Stretch of slow current, a water-bird
Heels, down-angles, touches. You are the one
Who sees the nerve-tremble of ripple, broken

Dusklight craze on the water as that body of light
Settles. You are the one the child
Comes to out of the rustmarked
Car you parked back on the highway,

And it is you who has to define
What is not fear but feels like fear
To this boy who does not want to understand
But wants you to be there, whole.

You touch his face. It is like touching
Someone years ago, man or woman,
Someone another age from you, whose life
Has nothing to do with yours, father or mother

Or light-bodied stranger come winding
On a tremble of air to settle it all, to settle.

v. *Domestic*

Raised to the light, the cut
Delphinium goes translucent,

Cleared by the sun of its pale
Milk-blue obscurity of bell-

Inflected blossom. The bed
You cut it from is choked with ragged

Second-year growth,
Untended biennial, half

Blighted, overrun
With unnameable weeds. One

Quick swipe of your file-honed hoe
Would clear the whole mess, and you

Promised it that way, but you stand
Holding the bloom-spike in one hand,

And it must be pure physical fact,
Consequence, cause and clear effect,

That a shaft of blue light falls
Against your face, light visible

Only in the plane
Of eye, blossom, sun,

Arc-light blue, the same
Light he came to you in: and you know him

By no known history, no
Shared name, but only that light through a window,

Only the hands that lifted
Your skirt, the voice that said,

21

Suddenly, *yes*—only you
Cannot be certain who,

In that venetian-blind-rayed
Angle of motel-room light, said

What. But no matter. What is known
Is the touch, that hand

Trembling inches from your face, its strange
Convolutions of flesh twice the age

You remember, holding, above the yard and its
Home-grown plot

Of entanglements,
The fresh-cut, unsingular

Flower. In this strong light
It is suddenly almost clear.

AN ABANDONED FARM IN THE WEST

This clear shadow shimmers on the side of a barn,
Heat-struck shape of an animal or rust-broken machine

No one remembers the name of: the body
Of a man who died passing through,

Some drifter no one knew, or wanted to.
No woman would have dreamed of marrying him.

And out there in the field that cattle no longer keep
Close-cropped, there is the edgeless shadow of a cloud.

If you stay here for half an hour, it will all be gone,
Made over by another angle of sun, and since it is no place

You know, you will not recognize it
As yours: the broken silo, the corral,

The farmhouse warped on the weather of its frame.
Somebody's father marked off this field, made it square,

Raised wheat bright as the forgotten hair
Of the daughter he would have loved

If it had all gone right, but his wife
Has locked him out of the house. He knocks, calls.

She is crying at the kitchen table, hunched
Inhumanly. He prays to be let in.

She mumbles *Heresy, heresy* and does not hear.
Anyone might have been born here, might have named

The light-jagged mountains thrown down in June sun,
Anyone among us might have scattered these small stones

In the oblivious story of our play while the woman sings
Her mother-song from the bedroom window

And the man drags his crippled foot in sheets
Of what he would have sworn would soon be snow:

Anyone might have loved anyone, anyone might have married
The first body come whistling down the slow-dusked road,

Anyone might be your brother, lifting the blue flowers
Of your dress in the corncrib's innocent dark:

And you love him as long as you can, hold on to the hard
Life he makes while he shivers in the heat

This shadow means, not knowing it is in you, torn
To the shape of a man in the field of your own failed season.

EMPTY BACKSTREET IN A SMALL SOUTHERN TOWN

The daughter who has never been here
Will make the connection. It will not be time
For the vine-grip of morning glory,
It will be the rainsilvered winter
You never hear much about, February,

And wind will blow raw down
The left side of a street the locals call
Main Street, Niggertown.
She will come here alone, dark-skinned
For a white girl, pitiful

In her unbelief. From the first
House she comes to, the unpainted tin-roofed
Wrack-frame shack, she will hear
Nothing, no hymn-singing mother-voice, no left-
Over cottonfield harmonica, no ghost

Of a pot-bellied white-eyed child
Squealing from a doorway. She would swear
On the whole street there is nobody
Home. This is not what she came here for,
This is not the story

She wanted: no: there will be nothing
To keep her rust-colored
Hair from blowing loose, nothing to hold
Back the blood-poisoning
Bite of this unexpected

Wind. In her grimace she will look
So much like her mother
It would break your heart if you had one,
If you could know her
Unspoken history of abandonment: but the sun

Will slap its ice-white
Presence on the blacktop,
And nobody will come to explain,
No mammy and no pistol-sagging cop,
Nobody will come to say what

Any of this means, or will ever mean,
In the unfolding human
Heresy of pain

—*for Jodi Baker*

CANCER RISING

a dream of walking

Maybe this has been done before. Light scatters
Over that ragged western edge of sky he knows
Is trees, hedgerow, wheatfield's boundary, the end of the family
Farm, a border taking on, in this moment's illumination,
The look of a black raw rip
In the tissue of the air,
                              so he knows it is evening.
He is walking. He has been walking
A long time, maybe hours, or it feels that way.
He does not seem to be going anywhere,
But that does not disturb him. It is winter,
Not a hard freeze, field the dim gold
Of frostbit straw.
                     In this light he could be hanging
From nothing, high in the mild luminosity of the sunset
Itself. He is wearing khaki, its tan the same
Shade as the field's, and he thinks he must be
Invisible here to anything watching,
Even the hard silhouettes of hawks
Turning and falling in the distance,
                                   disappearing, rising,
Appearing, heeling over the edge, out from the edge
Of that darkness under the sky. There is nothing
Strange about it. He knows this field. It is the land
He has lived on since he was a boy
Riding bareback on a led mule, hanging
Terrified and mute
                    to the hacked mane while the man
With the halter-rope in his hand laughed and would not stop.
He knows he was lifted up to straddle
The mule's high hard spine, knows he suffered like Jesus
In what he barely knew enough to call his balls
At every deliberate mule-step, jolted
Hard over that field of earth turned
                              by the plow for the planter.
But that was then. Now he is walking alone,
The mule dead and the man who led it dead
As Jesus, years. Now nothing lifts him up.

27

He walks on his own legs, painless, quick
As he ever remembers, no younger than he knows
He is, but strong, and he thinks
                    of the woman, thinks
How good it is, when it happens, to find himself suddenly
Able, even at their age, and to find it
As good as it was when they were twenty,
Just married, still childless and amazed:
Good as it was, it is still just as good to touch her,
Still just as good to rise
                    and enter
Invisibility, clear gold of field-light
With a clear sense of time, old enough now to know
What pain means, and what it means to have it
Gone. He turns and looks east, back toward the house with its high-
Ceilinged rooms and polish-blacked
Furniture they say is antique
                    but he knows is only old:
Knows his body lying there in its drugged sleep
Will tremble awake soon enough. She will
Touch his hand, and he will tell her
I had a beautiful dream. I dreamed I was walking.
When he sees her tears, he will regret that he has spoken.
She misunderstands,
                    she thinks it is a sadness
That the mind, dying, dreams what it leaves behind.
But he knows, as he stands looking back at the house lights
And the stars rising above them in the horizon's indigo quick,
That the worlds of dreams are always self created,
And if in his dying the world creates itself again
And gives him back his legs,
                    strong as they ever lifted him,
That is not grief. The body in that bed she sits beside
Waiting for him to wake regrets everything. But in his dream
He regrets only that he does not know the world so well
He could be sure every detail of it is true:
Grieves he does not know enough about the constellations
To say certainly that the one he sees
                    scrabbling its slow way
Over the roofbeam, the one he knows enough to call
By its true crab-name, is really where it ought to be:

Because if it is, its obvious symbolism is heavy-handed,
And if it isn't, the dream is all a goddamned lie.
But he finds he cannot remember. If he ever knew,
His memory withholds the answer.
                    And that is the one true pain,
That there is so much he does not know, like any man:
That out of the arrogance of men like me, who pretend to know
Anything at all only because they are so afraid of losing
Pain, because they want to go on and on
Touching the bodies of women and dying slow, but never dying,
Ambiguities come to be
                    rearrangements, ironies, mysteries, heresies
Of a man dream-walking a field, or a constellation
With a name that spreads in the breath-clear air
By starry clawpoints, moving dumb, hanging on,
Clinging and ripping at the bellowed lungs of the sky,
Slow-brained in its terror of being, or being lifted there and named
Anything at all by anyone,
                    living or dying.

CONVENTION: AN ALTERNATIVE

An opportunity. A choice. She sprawls across the bed
Like something thrown there. Bars of radiance invisible
Except to vision deeply dark-sensitive touch her now
Through half-open venetian blinds. Outside and down

Ten floors is Boston Common. Already people
Are there on the sidewalk. Some sit on a park bench
In March snow. I imagine them as aristocratic derelicts,
The best names in Boston brought, from where I watch them, low.

I can see them in the mingled arclight and dawnlight,
My right forefinger bending one metal blind-slat
Down in a gangster movie gesture. I am above
Those blue spheres of the streetlights. In this room overpriced

Even at convention rates, illumination comes from elsewhere.
I turn from the window and look at her again, marked
With her aura of darkness and light. This is temptation, friends.
I want to leave it at that. It would be the right thing.

But I am going on with it, looking at her,
Seeing her here as no one else will ever see her.
She is naked. She has thrown the covers back.
Fathers, brothers, this is when I need you.

I need your voices. Tell me what I've done.
She moves in sleep, her shoulders shift, her breasts.
Her hair on the pillow is colorless, light.
This is the present tense. There is nothing else,

Not even memory, except what I remember
Of her body, the peculiar texture the flesh
Of her nipples takes on when I touch it with my tongue.
All that is invisible now, but I see it

With my body, the same way I see the scene
Where the man on the park bench outside loses his birthright.
Something has happened. Someone does not approve.
There are arguments, ultimatums, disownings,

There are comings and goings. Somebody's heart is broken.
Somebody's will gets changed. What does it take, forefathers,
To turn a patriarch into a wino?
Different things, I guess, for different places and times.

She turns her head in sleep, and I see the nap
Of the ruined bedspread has lettered her skin
With its scarlet. This is not what I meant to give her.
There are times, I swear it, when guilt is nonexistent,

When anyone will do anything. My family has a story:
At sixteen, my grandmother wanted
To run away with a man three times her age.
They caught her at the edge of town and took her home.

She stayed in bed three weeks. They called it a sinking spell:
Now we would say *depression*. I imagine her lying there
Wondering what she has missed. There are times when guilt
Is everything, and there's nothing you can do.

In this room dawnlight, the world's final secret
Touch, a reason for everything, innocently grows.
Outside, on the street below, people are moving.
Going where? Why? Where have they been all night?

In houses all over this city, there are beds
Where the righteous married lay hands on each other, asleep
In their unconscious ease. They know who loves who
Is a fated thing. Ancestors, on their tongue, fate

Is a mouthful of strange flesh, a dark old word.

THE AFTERWORLD

One day it will all be clear
Why the brother who stayed behind
On the family farm didn't marry

Until he was forty, and then
It was his high-school sweetheart, the one
He put it to on a pick-up seat,

So good he couldn't forget.
Ashes to ashes, the preacher says,
And the first spade of dirt showers down.

We are all good Methodists singing
About the weak and the heavy laden.
He stands blond in his suit beside his wife

Who is pretty, who the years are kind to.
It is faith that leads to this,
A moment of transcendental vision

In the moonlit cab of a Ford,
Then the years of mortification
Of the flesh, the certain imagining

Of the hands of the man she married first.
We are almost all family here in our sorrow
At what things come to. The earth

Unpiles. Across the mound from me,
She touches his hand. They are somehow
So young it hurts, as though they stopped

In the middle of something years ago,
Fell gently together asleep,
And dreamed her two children with the dark

Hair of the other life.
Now they are singing here.
Their mouths move peacefully.

We have come to sing together
Over what we share,
Over what we wait for so long.

Whatever time has passed
Between us is done.
God loves you, the preacher says,

And someone alone turns quietly colder.
This is love and it matters,
It all works out.

II

Dogma

. . . certain themes recur in lower-class heresy. . . .
—CHRISTOPHER HILL

THE UNDERWORLD

Jefferson Island, Louisiana

White salt-glint
On the crystal curve of what is not sky
Where no stars are set

In any discernible infinity,
And out of the shadow-edge
Of these arclights' potency

Something comes moving, huge
And thunderous: earthmover,
Crawling a glittering bulge

Of firmament. Someone touches a lever
And it drops its load
In front of a gear-grinding Caterpillar

Our friendly guide confides
Was, like everything down here,
Dismembered and lowered

Through the same ten-by-ten-foot elevator
We dropped in by: a quarter mile
Subsurface. *There's a lake up there,*

He says, pointing at the ceiling, and while
He tells us the geological witchcraft
Of salt dome formation, I have metaphysical

Doubts. Which came first, the shaft
Or the machine?
How small can an earthmover make itself,

Even taken to pieces? I am nine
In this memory, no
Perfect tourist. I imagine

A squad of strong-men trying to
Cram a bulldozer blade through
An elevator door. It just won't go,

No matter how they angle it. And it seems so
Unworkable a story, like the Sunday school
Stuff about God and the Garden, too

Strange to be serious over: all
That trouble from nothing
But an apple? Adam that big a fool?

But everything seems unlikely: being
Here in the Salt Mines,
Floor, walls, ceiling

One impervious diamond-shine
Of what is in the process of becoming
Table salt: unlikely, being here again

In memory. I remember nothing
Of what was clearly a tedious
Journey, nothing of the road, nothing

Of the jokes my father wouldn't have tried to resist:
The Salt Mines, where they send
Bad communists,

Or where all poor bastards get the goddamn
Sweat they have to have on their brows to live by.
I recreate my father in his foolish imitation-

Tourist-hardhat, base-metal painted silvery-
Aluminum: *Regulation,* says our conscientious guide:
We have ours on, too, my mother and I.

Memory: I make them beautiful and good,
My parents, and they love me,
And here we are again with all the dead

Past. The guide is saying *Breathe*
In through your mouths. We do,
And come to life with the heavy

Taste of salt on our tongues. *It is so*
Strong in the air it condenses
In your saliva. Alive again, we go

Everywhere he tells us:
Up on a high glass-mound of crystals
Jackhammered out of the porous

Lake-water-rotted walls,
And against a brilliance only arclights
Can be throwing, I see them again in profile,

The human silhouettes they are, my parents, looking out
Silver-headed over the whole white hellish anthill
The guide says never stops, day or night,

And has not stopped, the tremble
In what passes for earth, for air,
This whole skull-

Hollow immensity full of the roar
Of memory's machinery.
My father and mother

Touch hands in the unknowing fear of lovers, and I
Hear the guide shout to me over the furious
Reverberation: *You should know, nothing we*

Bring down here can last:
They go soon: the salt, the humidity:
They rust.

THE IDEAL

CARDIFF GIANT: The world's greatest hoax:
made by a Chicago stonemason, buried on a
New York State farm and later exhumed, the
"Giant" in its time fooled hundreds of thou-
sands and is known in our history and legends.
　　　　　　—text from a postcard
　　　　　　bought in Cooperstown, N.Y.

North: the watered-down sun
Lets the light of its long life go
Shadowy over the spine
Of the Appalachians. Everything is old.

In the Rockies you want to believe
The planet has just been born,
Ragged cliff face and pure razor
Of switchback only this second ripped

Out of God's still unrevised dream
Of a place something unknown
Called humankind might live
Once the dust settles and the kinks

Work out of the idea of garden.
But these tame, torn-down mountains
Of the Northeast hardly seem Christian,
Too wind- and water-worn

To have been created at a stroke
Ex nihilo. Don't you believe it,
I can hear my grandmother saying.
Just because it's written down

In black and white don't make it so.
She had a face, her last
Years, like a washed-out field,
Eroded soil, not stone,

But that was in the level South
And she meant newspapers, not
Scripture or Emersonian stirrings
Of the soul over Nature's alphabet.

Nature to her was a farm,
And a farm was a wasted life,
But it was by God *her* life,
And she had no sympathy

For sanctimonious sentimentality.
1961: she points
To a headline. *Look here.*
These bleeding-heart Yankees

Are ruining this whole country
With their big ideas.
That's how I remember it.
But twenty-some years later, she's become

An idea herself. Days now
I've been driving in the cold
Peculiar light of northeastern summer.
I've stood on Mt. Holyoke squinting

Through smog at the hump of Monadnoc,
Have darkened in the shadow of the façade
Of Jonathan Edwards's reconstructed
Church on Northampton's square,

Then drifted west to Cooperstown
And the Susquehanna, where I lay late
In a motel room, trying to balance
A beer and the square mass

Of the *Norton Anthology* on my chest, reading
The first words of the sermon John Winthrop
Wrote on the *Arbella* in mid-Atlantic:
God Almighty in His most holy

And wise providence, hath so disposed
Of the condition of mankind, as in all times
Some must be rich, some poor, some high
And eminent in power and dignity,

Others mean and in subjection.
He was sailing in 1630
Toward a continent he had only heard of,
To found Eden in the august name

Of the Company of Massachusetts Bay,
And of course he called his sermon
"A Model of Christian Charity."
Now, near sundown, I drive straight

Toward the sun, away
From Cooperstown's Fenimore House
Where Cooper, that well-meaning ass,
Stares white-eyed from a big Platonic bust:

Drive away from the Farmers' Museum
With its blacksmith and weaver and endless
Display of artifacts tracing
The bloodline of the plow,

All on show in a barn
As elaborate as any cathedral,
Great curved beams with their woodglow
Against walls of medieval stone

Shining in loft door shafts of light.
Driving, I know now the names
And uses of outbuildings strange
To the South as Greek ruins: round

And polygonal barns, overgrown
Dutch barns, German barns, English barns
With Victorian gingerbread at the eaves
And widow's walks perched on the roof beam,

Functionless, vestigial.
These are not barns to me
But the idea of barn, unreal
And perfect, unattainable

To any farmer I ever knew,
Any farm I grew up knowing.
This is the country they came from,
Those people who haunted my people

With the shadow of hatred thrown
A hundred years: Yankees. These
Are the farms they lived on,
These are the barns their horses

Stamped and chafed in, blowing
Steam in winter air,
High-strung and hot to draw
Sleighs through landscape paintings

Of mythological snow, or charge
Breastworks at Bull Run and Shiloh.
Yankees, my grandmother said.
What do they know about us?

Her question drifts back to me
From 1961, a year
As distant as any in history.
I can't answer. The highway snakes

Through postcard upstate New York's
Edenic farms, and I am on it, lost
Except for the abstraction of map
Fading in dusklight on the car seat.

It is a problem in pure faith.
I am eleven. My grandmother,
Who I love, is shaking the headline
In my face. *What do they know*

About who we are? Who do they think they are
To try and change how we live?
I will know till the day I die
She was a good woman with ideas

So vile it hurts me to remember,
Not just because they were hers
And I loved her, but because they were also
Mine. *Nobody a thousand miles away*

Can tell us how to run things.
Our niggers know their place.
For my grandmother and for John Winthrop
Jefferson's self-evident truths

Were unnatural, ungodly, un-American.
They had their own clear notions
Of disenfranchisement and perfection.
We believe what we believe.

I believe something about this country
Turns good people into fools.
Just outside the door
Of the Farmers' Museum's impossible

Barn, I saw a lean-to built
Above a mound of earth, and lying there
A five-ton hunk of granite
Carved in the weird shape of a man.

Absurd as it seems, the whole
Nineteenth century thought the Cardiff Giant
Was a petrified human, one of us,
But larger than life. A sign

Said somebody buried it on somebody's
Farm, and when the fieldhands plowed it up
Like a freak potato, they fell to their knees.
It lies comic now under its shelter,

Legs cracked off, testicleless
Penis lacerated. But it smiles like a bad
Caricature of Adam the first morning of the Fall.
Staring down at it, I could have sworn

44

It knew it had been believed in.
P. T. Barnum believed,
And his faith sold tickets,
Not just for the Cardiff Giant

But for a dozen copies of it.
One year, its castoff images
Swept the whole country.
East of this highway, the good

Liberals of Boston tend
Their pre-Revolutionary houses
And the white middle class goes marching
To Boston Common against busing.

My grandmother taught me that irony, right
For the wrong reasons, too easy.
It took the flicker of police clubs
Falling on black and white

TV news to get me started
Sorting it out years later.
Tonight I'm still sorting. I believe
Human love evolves. But I'm stuck

With all I was born with, American.
We want to be larger than something.
We want to be more than ourselves.
It is dark. I turn my headlights on.

The shadows they cast span fields.

*—for John Hales
and Joe Battaglia*

THE REAL

Years before I knew about the Cave
Or those double-sexed science-fiction
Archehumans of the *Symposium,*
I first heard of him

On a second-grade field trip tour
Of my miserable hometown library
Where he was reduced to nothing

But a small white bust
Of marble (fake), a couple
Of terms (philosopher, Greek),
And that singular-sounding name

Alien as the name of a planet.
It was awesome. I had no idea
What any of it meant. But if a man

Could have his head turned
Into that smooth, undifferentiated object
On a dusty oak stand in a corner
Of a room full of books,

There had to be something behind it.
Nights I tried to remember
Plato's face on that bust

So I'd know him if I met him, or saw
His picture in the paper,
But it was useless. There was nothing
To imagine him by, and I grieved

The way you do when you forget
The face of someone you care about
Or deeply hate. Later on, he made me feel

Like a fool for not knowing
He was older than Jesus, and just
As dead. Jesus I knew about,
Since he was an obvious American

Institution. Jesus and I
Came to an understanding early on.
When I was seven, my eyes went bad,

Nearsighted, and I prayed for vision.
What I got was glasses. Ashamed,
I thought if Jesus thought
I was worth anything,

What I'd prayed for
Was a small enough favor.
I already knew the objections

To thinking that way:
You asked for the wrong thing.
You asked in the wrong spirit.
Jesus always answers your prayers,

He just says no sometimes.
That cut no ice with me.
What I wanted was real,

I believed in it, I needed
To see things clearly.
Do unto others, I thought.
But Jesus sees everything.

I know my theology was faulty,
But I was born in Mississippi,
A Methodist. My education was bad.

If Jesuits had brought me up,
I would have been different, I'm certain.
I would have known the reasons for human suffering.
I would have known who Plato was.

As it happened, all I had to go by
Was what passed in me
For common sense, and an imagination

Undisciplined and overactive.
By the time I was twelve, I'd confused
Plato and *Pluto* and *plutonium*.
It was 1962. We were going through

The Cuban missile crisis
When a girl in my science class
Started screaming: *There's going to be*

A war, we're all going to die.
The teacher calmed her down
And we prayed together, but I
Would not close my eyes.

We'd seen films of Hiroshima
And diagrams of nuclear explosives.
We knew about chain reactions and fallout shelters.

We knew that when the fireball comes
You look away. Maybe that girl's fear
Was what made me want to kiss her.
No, she said, *let's be platonic.*

I didn't know that soap-opera word.
I thought it meant dead. It worked.
It was like a force field

Or a terrible embargo.
Platonic love preserved me
Years in a dictatorial state
Of tortured virginity.

In the dark bedroom, my body glowed.
I could take off my glasses and see
In the night sky out my window

Not pinpoints of light, but cold
Distant balls of fire, white, unreal
As constellations, but unimagined, visible.
What does it mean that I became a shadow

In my own untrustworthy mind?
What does it mean I could only love
Other shadows like me?

The winter John Kennedy died
Some of my classmates cheered.
I didn't, but I didn't know
If it was right to grieve.

That's a hard thing to admit.
But I was confused. Those were confusing times.
The South had spent a century

Perfecting the purity of hate.
It was them or us, we said.
We hated the North, communists, Russians,
Catholics, Negroes, liberals and atheists

Everywhere. How could I know what to love?
Everywhere I turned I found a world
I was afraid to touch,

Unreal. If there was truth
It was somewhere else.
I knew it. Everybody knew it.
But no matter. That was our idea of heaven.

We were dying blind, turning into permanent shadows
Caught in some meaningless moment
Of what we prayed was not

The only life: burned childlike
Out of ourselves at any given instant
Of grace: touched by the fire, etched white
Against a pure black wall.

DOGMA: PIGMEAT AND WHISKEY

I woke in half-dark. There was smoke
That followed me.
I floated up choked on pin-oak, post-oak,

Water-oak, and just enough hickory
Burning. Somebody came,
Lifted me and spoke, whiskey

Mixed in that voice with my name:
Just the wind shifting, son.
Go to sleep. But the dream

I was having wouldn't have me back. He put me down
Away from the fire, on the other
Side of that smoke-cloud blown

Thick to the ground I had dreamed on, and where
The old man still sat
Silent in his straight-backed chair,

Ghostly in coalglow risen from the pit
Where the spitted pig sputtered
And leaked its vitriolic fat.

I could not see his face, but I knew the red
It must be turning
As he sat like the martyr he was, as he suffered

In silence, burning
At the stake of another indignity.
He's old, my father was always saying,

Old and proud and onery:
Too pigheaded to miss one more year
Of lording over what could only

Be called his family ritual. Wheelchair
Or no wheelchair, stroke or no stroke,
He was still himself, more or less, and so was here

To make sure they did it his way. I thought I heard him choke
On what was maybe pride and maybe outrage
Or maybe the dense suffusion of woodsmoke

They'd left him incensed in. *God help us! At his age!*
In his shape? my uncle had said, and my father:
You know as well as I do what he wants. It was obvious knowledge,

Plain as a wart on a nose, clear
As revelation.
So, my uncle said, *We got to. Yep,* said my father.

And now he sat half-forgotten
And half-asphyxiated by the fire which by God he
Himself was the one

Had taught them how to build. And now it fell to me
To say something, since it looked like
I was the only one who could see

The old man vanish as the smoke came over him thick
On night wind turned suddenly contrary.
I'd like to be able to remember myself think

Goddamn it, I'm only seven. Why me?
I didn't, so I can't. But I know I knew things were
Not what they had been or what they ought to be.

Even my being there
Was a breach of the old decorum
I'd never thought about before

But understood in violation as soon as I saw them
Roll him across the yard that evening
Into the south pasture and lift him

Out of the wheelchair, fierce in his uncomplaining
And unforgiving silence. They set him in his rocker by the pit
Where he could suffer what they were doing

To his fire and his pig all night,
Not able even to bite his own stroke-locked tongue.
Son, he used to tell me, *I'll tell you something and you remember it:*

Two things by God's will belong
To any man, no matter who he is: his fire and his wife:
Any man who messes with either one is not just wrong,

He's a yellow-livered lowlife.
Sure as I'm living, those are words any *man can live by.*
He was mistaken, but I didn't know that, any more than I knew grief

Has to do with more than dying. I thought dying was plenty
To be sorry about. I thought the old man was a goner. I didn't know
What that meant, but I was right. It was easy

To be right about: he was ninety-seven years old,
Born in 1860, the first year of the Civil War.
He remembered things. They came out in stories he told

Over and over until nobody wanted to hear:
How, at the end, the Yankee soldiers came, and he sat
On a split-rail fence shouting *You killed my father*

As they marched in the July dust. In fact, they were innocent.
His father died in a prison camp of typhus,
And after the war, a Northern philanthropist lady brought

His personal effects all the way from Washington, a long and dangerous
Journey in those days, especially for a woman alone.
Stories, stories: he told them to us,

And we listened, the same ones again and again.
God knows we were bored, but we remembered
Things he never even said. I have dreamed that scene:

He sits, five years old, his face transmogrified
By this illusion of false memory into mine:
He shouts, and the soldiers turn their known heads,

Powder-smoke-blackened and shell-scarred in a dream's
Heavy-handed imagery of war, to see
Who recognizes, who dares to name

The act committed in the sight of all humanity,
The sudden blood on their hands
Melodramatic as dreams, I suppose, have to be.

I dreamed that as a boy, and have dreamed it as a man.
You killed my father: his voice says it and says it,
And the soldiers' faces, of course, are ours. Now I understand

How obvious it is. In that night,
The family was gathering around him
Like smoke, blowing in from everywhere. I remember it

As the last of our great reunions. They were always the same:
Every Fourth of July we bivouacked like the small army
We were, all over his drought-burnt front lawn,

Ate potato salad and pigmeat while he
Sat stiff and unmoved in his cane-bottomed porch rocking chair
Proclaiming it again and again: *I*

Started all this. That was dogma. And the night before,
The men stayed awake by the pit they'd dug
In the scorched afternoon to hold the fire

And the corn-fed carcass of the great old hog
They'd quaintly spitted, not for the redneck mystique of the thing,
But so we'd all have enough to eat. I used to beg

To stay up with them, but nothing
I said would ever persuade my father
Until this time. He didn't even give in:

It was his idea. And being there,
Seven years old, I knew being there was worthless.
It didn't mean what it would have meant before

The stroke, before the paralysis
That left my great-grandfather silent,
Fierce, ridiculous, too helpless

In his misplaced chair even to shout
At my uncle and my father for drinking whiskey,
Which he, a hard-shell Baptist, hated—it meant

Nothing at all about me.
It meant that old man was dying.
It meant that old man's family

Was about to begin unraveling.
What is it I'm trying to say here? I know I sound
Like just another Southern storyteller telling

Another Southern story about the war, that Dark and Bloody Ground,
Family, memory, history, old men, time.
Everyone's sick of that, me included. Once Pound

Wrote, with characteristic wisdom
And a dogmatic sneer *The narrative impulse is a product
Of the village mentality.* I can't argue with him.

I can only mutter *If it's so, then so be it.
But what the hell else is there!*
My great-grandfather's voice says it and says it:

I started . . . you killed. . . . And I can't help but hear
How I said *Daddy: Great-grandpaw:*
I can't help recreating my father

Turning and squinting in the firelight until he saw.
Look here, he said to my uncle, *we're smoking Grandaddy.*
Even the names: *Daddy, Grandaddy, Great-grandpaw:*

Hopelessly provincial. The village mentality
With a vengeance. But it's what we all said.
And they stood on each side of him then, breathing whiskey

In his outraged face: they lifted
His dying body, in clumsy love, gently.
He rose in that smoky firelight like the image of God—

Smoke, the old folk wisdom says, *follows beauty*—
Spitted and upthrust on his provincial mortality.
I saw it. It's all I've got, on my honor, my sole authority,

As good, I guess, as anyone's: a witnessing, a story.

—for Fred Chappell

III

The Undersoul

> . . . it was the grey sea that bore you
> and the towering rocks, so sheer the heart in you
> is turned from us.
>
> —HOMER

THE FUTURE

Portico, colonnade, tiled hallway
Open on the left to rain,
It will be clean-swept as the scene
Of an accident: as if they

Have already come with hoses, pushbrooms,
Scoured the stains.
New to this, you will lean
Hard on my arm,

Will walk with a strange
Lightness, trying to quiet
Your tileslick echoes, indiscreet
Footsteps, not to interrupt the pain

Of two dark lovers leaning
In a column's shadow.
Every shuttered window
We pass will have a saint's name shining

From a small brass plaque, patrons
Of months, days, hours,
Their Spanish titles prayers
Against time. We will imagine

Their cells inside, the clean
Sandstone floors,
Squat handcarved chairs
Still set beside worn iron

Beds: and on the walls
Near corners, waist-high sockets where
Kneeling men ground their foreheads years
In fits of mystical passion. All

Their lovelike moans
Are silent already: and we
Will be tourists in that scenery,
Our lives that much more gone,

Maybe white-haired, looking out
An archway at the shock-sheen
Of desert heat waves, the unknown
And unforgiving sky about

To take on its first night stain
As we stand the same
Woman and man, touching
Cold stone, minute by minute remembering

The future of our own
Blood-darkened and vanishing names.

THE SECOND STORY

On the other side of the arc-light-level window
Hung at the top of that slope of Victorian porch,
Someone believes in the laying on of hands,

Or some two believe, and the woman of them sings
Her hymn. It comes down to me where I stand unashamed
To listen, unashamed to be here under these morning stars

Where they do not know I am, where no one should be.
This is the life in the body, certainty, uncertainty:
I am here, and if they knew, they would not be

What I imagine so easily, the woman a darkness
In the shadow the man above her casts, starlight and arclight
From the window by the bed eclipsing his face from her,

Her legs lifted around him in that delicate poise
Of the almost-come, so when he lowers
His invisible mouth that could be any man's

And takes her breast, her knees stiffen in the same
Upward motion that suddenly and beautifully breaks
This contralto out of her, as the freed light strikes

Her face: that, or some familiar variation. But if they knew
Another darkened body stood on the innocent
Corner of two sidewalks below them, listening,

What would they be? I ask myself and know:
Up there in that bedroom I can almost see
With its various reproductions—armoire, nightstand, vanity,

Surrounding its crucially refinished bed—
They would, if they could suddenly know me, stop
Their singular motion in the paralyzed reflex of fear,

Afraid, God help me, of nothing, of me,
A human stranger. So knowledge is fear.
I look up at the house spreading its white façade

Streetlight-struck in the blackness of this summer morning,
Five A.M., Vermont, windless and cloudless,
And I see, I want to tell myself simply,

A house. But I know it is no house
I ever lived in. These are the second homes
Of the rich, on a street of stained glass and cupolas

And high balconies where a clichéd lover might declaim
Wherefore? and the answer rise *What light?*
And where lawns of tame maples yield

That storied Vermont sweetness: sap.
I have come here insomniac, waked by a dream
Not frightening, but strange in its inexplicable

And boring complications, the way the mind is,
And I remember the old joke: *The rich
Are not like us*, it goes, to which the answer is

The only one possible: *Right, they have more
Money.* I imagine those two up there, after,
Smoking identical Turkish cigarettes while he tells her

The details of an obscure incident from his childhood.
She nods in the dark and explains. After all,
Her Ph.D. is Viennese and psychological

And ought to do her some good in what she likes
To call her *private life.*
Yes, it is good to lie in the dark and breathe

That alien smoke through bruised lips, good to imagine
The love lives of distant and exotic peoples
In inner-city Detroit or Mississippi

And how, unexamined and mentally unhealthy,
They must hurt each other. And yes, it is good
To stand on the sidewalk hearing it go on and on,

That utterly unknowable woman transcendentally moaning
Out of a life I can only pretend to imagine,
And which I tell myself I could cause

To come to a crashing *coitus interruptus* by a single
Shouted word. Any word would do: *me*
I could yell, or *here,* or *Detroit,* or *dysfunction,*

It would all be the same word: *fear.*
So words are fear, as long as they let us know
Someone is out there, someone is close by, present

And mysterious in a body that has a familiar shape
But no known face. This is the life
In the body, what we know of each other, the nothing

Names tell us: this is the song
Of the woman touched by the man she thinks
She knows or loves or her life

Would be nothing without
Touching in rooms so dark nobody can say
Who anybody really is, where nobody has

Words songlike enough to touch
The reason I am out here, afraid
Of whoever is up there, lifted

In their Victorian construct
Over the world they speak to without knowing,
Moaning down their wordless and irrefutable explanations,

Giving hands and tongue to name me
Their human groping, making
What even the most petrified among us certainly

Could agree to call *love,* could say
Is good. But now her low voice rises
Toward a classic soprano. I feel its pure

Shudder low in my spine as she tells me
What I translate roughly as *My God*
Someone is doing something right:

And I know I have missed my chance, they are beyond me,
Too far gone for any word
I could shout ever to bring them down.

This is the rapture, these are the sinless
Raised beyond the reach of any voice
Of mine. This is salvation, I am forgiven

My fear and my dreams: I am foretold,
In this flesh that holds me, wherefore
What light (it is the east) grows suddenly unashamed

On the other side of trees that are only
Eclipses of themselves, thrown hard on the edge
Of this world's unnameable laying on of richness.

THE SUN

Something is happening in the garden. The woman leans
Over ragged rosebushes raggedly trained
On a low wood fence. Her breasts, in the flower-embroidered
Linen of her halter top, reveal

A plumb bob's sensitivity to gravity, the deep
Crease between them a hard right angle to the crease
Her bending crimps in the off-white plane of her belly.
She reaches. She touches the buds' reddening tips.

You think I think this is Eden, don't you? I don't.
I think this is sex. I lie
On the lounge chair, balance my Budweiser bottle
Right-angled on this belly that years of beer

Would leaven and lift like yeast
If I ever gave up the old war against excess of flesh,
And I watch her. I think this is good. I think
Something is happening. It comes to me

With the irreducible momentum of the involuntary:
Late afternoon, a summer Saturday,
I am lying on my bed, where the sun
Through a window throws its hard-edged light:

I am having the first conscious sexual fantasy
In my memory. There is a stage, far away:
I am sitting, perhaps, in a balcony,
Or maybe I am simply hovering in the air,

High up, and distant from the action.
Onstage, a tiny woman takes
Her clothes off, piece by indistinct piece.
That's all. It's unrealized and conventionally abstract

As anyone's painful first poem, but for now it's enough:
I am nine years old, and I suddenly know a secret
Knotted connection between mind and body:
The center of the sunlight's hot rectangle

And my solar plexus coincide, squaring the circle,
And just below that geometry, my hard-on makes a chafed
Right angle: penis, ghost finger that will not answer
Directly to orders, as hands do, has answered:

And to what? To the image of breasts, however
Unclear: to the naked image of the woman
Moving in her faraway dance, removing
Only what stands between us most superficially,

Bending, when it's over and nothing else matters,
In a deep ironic bow. This is my first knowing. I lift
My beer bottle, look through it, and see her refracted
At two removes: from my far seat

In the balcony, or the place where I hang
In the air like an angel: and from here in the hot
Backyard where I lie in the sun turning red,
Where everything is happening, where you bend

And let me imagine the line between your breasts
Abstractly extended to intersect the belly-crimp
Exactly at your navel, crossing the two
Planes and four corners of the world at the arc

Of the solar plexus, the thousand-petalled lotus,
The rose that unfolds in summer when the sun
Touches it there, at noon, in the garden,
Whatever name you want to give it,

Whatever you know it by: uncontrollably risen.

THE IMMORALITIES: DRUNK ALL AFTERNOON

Light on the glass-topped tables, light on the lake,
A pale skein of charcoal smoke lifting over the scene:
It could all be as elegant as a Florentine fresco,
It could give off the odor of old velour
If whoever is in charge of the vision has a taste for that,
But you'd have to leave out the woman. Her swimsuit
Has shrunk oddly since she borrowed it last year
From her sister, who is just her size,
And now she is embarrassed that her body
Reveals itself in the fleshy distortion she hates
On other women. And you'd have to leave out the boy
Who sits on the sand by the water
Whining to go home.
                    Smeared on the far shore
Half a mile away is a pale line of oaks. The tint
Of their leaves is various. You could make something of it.
You nearsighted ones: take your glasses off and let it blur.
Impressionism reinvented. Or lift up your tumblers:
The light in your gin and tonic is so Platonically clear
You imagine the astral body must be like this,
The intensity of the soul's essential core
As tangible, all of a sudden, as your limes' burnished green.
It's funny how, such moments, we think of ourselves
In the plural: blurred you, royal We.
                                    These are moments
Of our most intense solitude, when we make up
Elaborate stories about the cast-iron furniture
On the restaurant's veranda, what it says when no one's around.
We know, with the certainty of inspiration,
It converses in French.
                        Up and down the beach
Fathers are shouting. I can hear their voices
And the voices of children screaming back.
I don't know what they are saying. Not far from me, the woman
Tugs at the bottom of her swimsuit. God help her, her body
Has abandoned her, and the boy mouths
Something that sounds, perhaps, like *nobody loves you*
As, far out on the lake, on that clarity of water,
A skier turns upside down, falling, utterly without sound.

IN SHOCK

I want to love this city, love these boys
Who come out of the elaborate loneliness of the Port Authority
With brushes and buckets, yelling at cars pulled up
At stoplights *Wash ya winsheel fra buck, Buddy!*
But I know that's too easy to love, exotica, like the noise

Of subways rising suddenly out of grates:
Like this old black man in his slick suit and trimmed goatee
Who lies on the sidewalk passed out or dead.
One way or the other, he is laid out straight,
Formal as a sarcophagus, his fifth of whiskey

Clasped two-handed over his heart. He guards it like a rose.
It's too easy to say his face is beautiful, that it glows
In its high octaroon bronze like a saint's,
That a small gold ring lifts its glitter from the flare of his nose.
It's true enough, but any fool knows

Nine times out of ten the truth is unbelievable.
Sometimes I feel this way. I want to love
Everything. I come to, now and then, the way I remember
Waking up certain spring mornings when I was a child,
Knowing I could love whatever I wanted. I could have,

But somehow it never worked out. I could never decide,
And then I'd forget. I was perverse.
That's the way those things always go.
The hero loses it. And now, nothing but a tourist,
I watch this old drunk sleep off his long suicide.

Or call it accident. But I cannot even see
The tremor of a dream cross his eyelids. In the August sky
Low clouds burn the color of mercury,
And a 747 detonates toward LaGuardia. I want to say
42nd St. is a sudden avenue into memory,

But it would be a lie. There is nothing here but this,
Nothing but heat and stink rising
From cars, gutters, warehouses, sweatshops, the whole
Undeniably human crowd of us.
All I remember is an amblance raising

Its pure nervous dissonance in another street. But that
Is happening now. The drunk twitches alive, leans
His whiskey bottle against the wall, sits up and smiles.
His blessing is angelic. Across the street, a magnificently fat
Italian woman scrubs a storefront window. Her husband

Comes out, crosses himself, starts
Shouting at her. *Now*, he yells, *now. Make it clean.*

THE UNPOETIC

On Being Asked, Whence Is the Flower?
—after Emerson

It is easy in time to forget
How the depth of dusklight rolls
Over these soybean fields,
Breaker-like, dense, green,

And remember instead the old farmer,
My uncle, who told me *Shit,*
We'll all be finished, boy,
If we don't get rain.

I'm tempted to just let that much stand,
As if making two unlike ideas
Fit a single broken breath
Were a big enough thing to do.

But I want it both ways at once.
I want everything. I want to say
I've gone back to that farm
I grew out of years ago, no farmer

By nature. I want to make myself
Visible, standing on the turnrow in light
Slanting through Southern air
So humid I might as well be underwater.

I can't stop this wanting now. That uncle is dead.
Something in his lungs
Ate out his breath, his voice.
You'd think that was final enough.

But light washes over me.
I think *Sea-change.* If I believed
In a spirit separate from the body,
I'd want it to look like this.

It would be pretty to imagine
We went that way, in a tide
Of subaqueous luminescence rising at sunset
Over anybody's best cash crop.

That's all it is, the soybean,
A broad-leafed insignificant-flowered
Concretion of a plant,
Not like the rhodora Emerson talked to

The way I would a woman.
He thought the flower symbolized the soul.
My uncle would have said that was crazy,
But he knew things Emerson never dreamed of.

Look, I make him say, *the soybean stands*
For money, and that's what it gets you
If you live that long, if you believe
In this dirt and sky enough

To sell your soul for rain.
I don't have even that much faith.
All I have is a life, another voice,
Light. And it won't last.

WELL-BEING

Tonight the western moon scatters its brassy tarnish
Over the tilted face of the pasture where junked machinery rusts
In the brush by the empty dog run: chisel-plow, hayrake, Amish
Horse-drawn cultivator with a fractured axletree, twists
Of rotted barbed wire gone backwards down the Great
Chain of Being until its strands are impossible to distinguish
From the iron-colored brambles that weave it all and warp it
Formally to the earth. Standing in this moon-thrown
Shadow of abandoned barn, I listen for the decorously hurt-
Sounding nightcall of an owl, but it does not come. I want pain
To be the subtext of this landscape, but nothing is real
In my scrap-metal-dappled and hopelessly overgrown
Field of vision except what my body insists is the concrete and literal
Shape of one fenced piece of world spun hard into autumn.
Two hundred yards away, down the slow landfall
Of what years ago passed as a real Ohio farm,
Small colored Chinese lanterns arc gently from maple to maple, mark
The yard where twenty or so moderately good friends have come
For the last lawn party of the year. They drink and talk
Under masses of star-shaped leaves that no one among them can see are touched
With the season's first color, a hard blood shade in the trees' clumped dark.
I am one of them, but I walk away, imagining the starkly hunched
Figure of the last old patriarch who plowed this field. Descended
Of the grandsons of Anabaptists, he sweated in his black clothes, he hitched
Modest workhorses to the honest machines God decreed, he minded
The commandments and his own good business on this earth, he loved
His wife and lay with her in her proper season, he ended
His life as he began it: with nothing, and in great pain. But nothing is proved
By what I imagine. In the yard behind me, someone touches a guitar,
And its random music hovers on the edge of my hearing, human, received
For what it is by nothing in this night not also human, no owl, no stone, no star,
Not even the moon, though its half-light fools me. I stumble on what I believe
Is one of its shadows, but underfoot turns real: earth-gouge, an old plow-scar.

—for Bob Cantwell

THE LOST

It gossamers in the air like the crystal thread of drool
That dangles from a baby's lip, or it prisms like that single
Strand of spiderweb suspended from tree to tree
I walked into at dusk once and felt how the beautiful clings:
High over Ohio, the near-vanished stream of a jet.

This is a problem in point of view, the way the world
And the things of the world reduce to abstraction or resist it.
From here and now, even direction is uncertain.
East to west, west to east: it was going one way or the other.
Everything is. I watch that vapor gauze in the clear air.

It tracks, like cloud-chamber light, some invisible motion
Until its afterimage doubles in my hard staring.
It's a wish like the will to live or the will to die
That makes me wonder where they are heading, whoever
Was up there. It turns me into one of them, the common desire

To be somebody somewhere else. From this small-town sidewalk
Across the street from a church I have never been inside, my angle
Of vision rises however high the zenith of the sky might be
To touch that streak of white laid out like a scar on a woman's belly,
Falling from the lip of the navel down the curve that outlines the globe

Of the uterus, where they cut her open and lifted
The baby out, the glittering scalpel navigated by compass points
Exactingly. Everything I see takes its place
On the metaphysical grid of heaven that after dark will yield
Constellations. But for now, I walk in this midwestern town

I do not know, past the churchyard where the rotten stone
Grave-markers lift their clumsy excuses: *Dead
Of Childbirth, Typhoid, Drowning, Life's
Terminal Self-Consciousness, Self-Reproach.* Somewhere, hung
Over another hidden circle of the earth, the jet holds

Secret clickings of gyroscopes inside its sleek hide,
And the navigator whispers at his headset like a lover. But from here
That white gouge in the sky is almost invisible, a fatal mark I see
Only when I look precisely elsewhere, telling myself
From all the other things of the world by its shimmering drift of obliquity.

COURSE OF EMPIRE

North America, 1985

I try to remember it happen:
               the predawn morning
With its cloudbanked starlessness spinning
Empty behind my windshield's
Headlight-tinted blank—the nausea of feeling
Nothing catch under the quivering
Fishtail skid of my old VW van
                    when I lose it on a stretch
Of invisible ice. I want the romance of panic,
But it's too quick for fear. When I lift my hand
In the amber flash of the hazard-lights
And thumb the universal signal of the stranded
To anyone willing,
               there is none of the outcast's shame
Or the terror of the lover
Whose adrenaline level tells him he has skidded
Up to the dark edge. It's only a snowbank
I'm stuck in, trying to remember what it means
To be a man who knows
               he is almost about to die.
It's 5:30 A.M. on a two-lane county road.
It's snowing on country already drifted
Two weeks deep. I give my gloved hand to the passing
Cars, which do not stop. I'm surprised
How many there are.
               I would never have imagined
How the wind of their passing pearls the air
A half-inch over the highway with delicately lifted snow.
But I would have never imagined any of this:
To be standing in shotgun range
Of a catatonic farmhouse, derelict, stuck,
                  thinking *This
Is Ohio winter and I'm just passing through here, boys,
I'm a stranger on my way someplace strange,
Somebody give me a hand.*
Thumbing the air, I might as well be praying
To the old indifferent God
               who scudded over on the *Mayflower*
And settled deep in the self-invented soul

Of the country. One of the elect?
That's not what I mean by fate. I mean being nobody,
Being nothing, so when the four-wheel drive
Pickup pulls off on the roadside,
                              it's a miracle:
I'm as stunned as the Indian who saw
The first gullwing of sail lift itself
Out of the horizon-edge of what he thought
Was world. *Ride to a phone?* I ask the driver
When he rolls his window down.
                              Hell, son,
I can pull you out. His voice is the voice
Of anyone's forefather, anyone
Palefaced and patriarchal who believes
In himself, who'd rather die fighting
Than stand by watching
                    even the most suspicious
Of his fellow Americans give up and call a tow truck.
It means he has to help me, no matter who I am.
It means he has to own everything
Either of us needs: shovels, jacks, chains.
It means he is fated to drive
                         the magnificent hugeness
Of his brand new pickup into the fading beam
Of my un-American van and hook
His rusty umbilical tow chain on my axle housing.
This is predestination, the irresistible
Mechanism of the universe
                         binding us into one
Strange vehicle revealed to passing drivers
As an incomprehensible darkness silhouetted
Snow-struck in Ohio sunrise.
We gun our engines, we shift, and I feel
The shiver of power surround me,
                              I stiffen to the truth
Of the law that says God loves the strong
And they will inherit the earth if there's anything
Left of it by the time the meek die out.
His pickup digs, moves, dislocates the weight
My van is. I lift

in the pure vicarious force
That otherness transmits to me along the frozen
Iron of our linkage, and I know for a moment
There is no death, I was right not to be afraid
When I felt my connection to the earth
Slither and vanish.
                        How could I die?
How could any of us ever die
Out of a world that has such power in it?
I am rising, nearly resurrected
From that mound of snow the momentum
Of my blind skid vanished into,
                              I am ripping free
Into the world that is mine by right,
By strength, by self-evident truth, by life,
Liberty, the pursuit of happiness, everlasting.
Am I praying? I don't know, but through the glittering spray
His wheels kick up, I make out the truth
                              of another, indifferent law:
As my van's rear swings, the pickup takes an equal
But opposite, uncalculated but obvious arc
Into the ditch I'm leaving, the two masses pivoting
Frictionless in a slow-motion pinwheel on ice.
I'm out, he's in,
            and the weight and force of my spin
Buries his back wheel to the bumper.
We're beyond irony now. We've come to destiny, manifest.
He shifts and guns and rocks himself in deep. Free,
I open my door and hear him shout
Red-faced, not at me
                  and not in wonder,
But into the hard air of North American winter,
His engine strangling, his breath pillaring the word
From his mouth: *Goddamn, Goddamn:* the only thing
We ever define as fate in the land of the free,
Cast out now in perfect impersonal thanks
                              for nothing, dying.

—*for David Baker*

HERESIES, OVERHEARD

At the corner church, colored light cantilevers harsh
Against this winter night through the body of Christ crucified
In stained glass. The heavy-handed
                                        lead lines that define
His suffering shape show black in the relief of absolute contrast.
He fluoresces above the invitation of an open double door
Where some carpenter framed him up
                                        as the architect planned, exact
And clichéd in translucent mimesis of flesh. Inside
It's prayer meeting night and they sing all together,
Maybe a hundred voices
                            skewed in their Protestant unison.
You want to talk theory, you want to talk the beautiful
And dangerous discipline of strictured harmony?
You've come to the wrong place, brother.
                                        Here they all believe
In the singular voice, here they make one note
Stand for everything. Where I am it's night,
And the myths say dark brings evil,
                                but this time it only brings me,
Strolling the root-heaved sidewalk, happy and going nowhere.
It brings a great cold sky full of the unflinching light
Of winter stars, which are not arranged
                                in lopsided dot-to-dot
Cave wall drawings of animals or gods. As far as I can see,
Which straight up is pretty far, they tell no stories.
Tonight all the beautiful and dangerous
                                stories are gone,
All passed from me: the one about the woman, about the boy I was,
About me, mother, father. It's cold, and my breath is a Christ-colored cloud
Of human steam where I stand
                            in my brilliant angle of churchlight.
That fact, now, is all I am. Above me, the stigmata
Are perfect circles of clear bloodred. Sweet Jesus died
At the hands of storytellers.
                            There was one who told us
Christ never suffered, his body was unreal. That was a heresy,
The critics said. They gave it a name and a dark denouement.
Every body's a critic, even the preacher's,
                                which quavers its off-
Key tenor against the perfect pitch of electric organ. The song he sings

Elucidates his text. And it's true: to have no flesh
Is to have no voice in the matter.
                       That's why I stand
Silent here between starlight and glasslight. The stories
Are lifted, vanished, even the one I like to call my life.
They'll be back, but for now I'm plotless,
                              and even the body fades
To dark as I walk on, happy, self-forgotten, whistling a random tune
Nameless and unrepeatable, but whose rhythm is the wrenched and real
Shape of the sidewalk and the way I stumble on
                               my own amazing grace.

THE COLD

a study in pushed time

You will see what looks like light
But is only the snow-broken
Air of February, Oklahoma night,
Moon- and starless. Yes: again:
The world of the hayfield ice-sparked
And naked and known.
Years from now, you will have parked
Your ruin of a Ford at the edge
Of some back road and walked
Just this far. Your age,
Then or now, is and will be
Unimportant. In that wreckage
Of ice-stubbled earth, you will see,
Where you stand expecting
Nothing, the white clarity
Of snow-scum on just freezing
Tilth, soil only now
At the sticking point. Breathing
That mysterious visibility of snow,
You will need to hear what I have to tell you:
You are not the blurred or universal you:
This is no rhetorical trick: I am talking to
Someone particular: I
Do not define you, though
In this world unexpectedly
Seen in the illusion of snowlight,
You cast no shadow. Listen: you will be
Cold, a little. You might
Hunch your shoulders while you stand
Waiting. All around you the night
Will be one inhuman
Ice-hiss. You will not know
Why you have come, or understand
That small muscle-jerk just below
Your left eye, there
Because you are staring so hard into
What ought to be dark, but is everywhere
Around you the world's falling and impenetrable glow.

■

Water, the teacher is saying, *possesses*
Strange characteristics: but I am staring
Across the room at the impossible breasts
Of a cheerleader, whose name I forget. She is wearing
A tight school-color sweater,
Chews gum with fierce concentration: the tearing
Of her teeth into the shapeless gray matter
Half a day's jaw work reduces Juicy Fruit to
Gnaws at the base of my spine. *Water,*
The teacher is saying, *behaves peculiarly: no*
Other substance expands when frozen: this
Is due to a unique molecular bond. So
What: I see her face
In profile against the black and white
Of the periodic table, know the kiss
Her mouth gives air as she chews is not
Mine and never will be: know she is this classroom's
Pure incarnation of beauty. So what:
I want her: and I feel the disgrace of my own
Inevitable expansion. *One centigrade degree*
Above freezing, the teacher is saying, *there is a sudden*
Contraction to maximum density:
The hydrogen bond collapses.
In that moment of opposed forces, he stares at me,
A small and reasonable man everybody says
Is queer as a three dollar bill.
Where, now, does he fasten his suspicious gaze?
You may find this dully theoretical,
He tells me, *but all this attraction and repulsion,*
This drama played out on the molecular level,
Has real consequences. Right: erection
Vanished, I stare at him my best stare
Of unadulterated hate, which slides off as the cheerleader yawns,
Looks down at her fingernails. Her hair
Burns elemental gold. *The abstract*
And the concrete, the teacher is saying, *are harder*
To separate than you may imagine, a fact
Among other facts you must get used to if you are
To understand the nature of things. She arches her back:
Her breasts loom inevitably: and, dear God, somewhere
The teacher is saying *So what, friends? So*

For instance, at the freezing point, water
Expands suddenly into, for instance, the tritely familiar
And abstract and inhumanly beautiful six-sided purity of snow.

■

Which rattles, for instance, on the window
Of a basement apartment in Utah, past midnight, where
A man and woman lie in the dark, in the slow
Black passing of time. Neither sleeps, and neither
Knows the other is awake. The man
Turns his head quietly, looks at the contour
Of her body against the gray square of the window. When
She does not move, he rises, goes
To pull back the curtain. The eye-level lawn,
Lit by a streetlamp, rises
In a bluish swirl. Now, he does not remember
That golden-haired abstraction of girl: the window freezes
His fingertips lightly to its frosted surface, and he wonders
Exactly what it was that bastard of a teacher said
About snow, about clear and miraculous structure,
But finds he cannot think, finds instead
And to his own astonishment he is crying, the clarity
Of tears suddenly cold on his face. *Dear God,*
He whispers, *what's this? What's the matter with me?*
Which the woman on the bed, for instance, has to hear,
But he does not know that. She does not say
Anything. His skin glows in the weird
Blue illumination of arclight, and she sees
The sudden icy shining appear
On his face, sees the inhuman beauty
Of his body, naked in the distance of that room:
It could be the beauty of any body,
Contour of flesh on impersonal schematic of bone:
And she wants to be touched, but does not
Want him to touch her: no: not him or anyone.
She turns on the bed as he watches the blue-white
Random motion of snow. He does not know his own
Fear, how it comes to him in this snow-flickered light:
A cold sweep of hair: the gold-bright
Chemical apocalypse of passion.

■

Years later, I returned
To the town I grew up in
And accidentally learned
In a casual conversation
How that bastard of a teacher died
After three decades of outliving
The woman he married
And who one day inexplicably drove
Her car off a bridge. Suicide
Or accident: no one could prove
Anything either way. *Unstable,*
Somebody said. *I heard from a cousin who lives . . .*
But that was all
Years ago. What I remember is how
They say they found him in the brutal
Cold of a February blizzard, too
Drunk to stand up, dying. He
Grinned at them when they brushed snow
From his face, said *Sorry*
To do it like this, men. Didn't mean
To be such a goddamned cliché.
So the story goes. He lived alone
For thirty years, a stranger in this
Town he came to, refusing to explain
Anything except the rigorous
Abstraction of natural law
And its beautiful deviousness.
Unstable. These things happen,
Soap opera or not. I know
The story is true, though it is almost
All now in the past.

■

Which is why, when you come here again, you will see
Light where there is no light:
You will come here completely
Alone, telling yourself you have been right
To do what you have done,
That solitude is the laboratory of the heart.
This is your inevitable destination,
This Oklahoma hayfield

Where you will stand, ignorant, human,
Not knowing yet the hole in your theory: *the real*
Boundary between hypothesis and truth
Is pain. It will be cold. You will feel,
Underfoot, the earth
Firm up. This is the freezing point.
This is the moment when snow and soil and breath
Are suddenly the same white
And everything is falling together:
Now and only now can I say in cold straight
Abstraction what I know you will need to hear:
You are a poor self-damned fool
Like everybody else. And you will hear the far
Bark of some idiot farm dog, will
Imagine that is what you came here for,
Will begin to feel
Foolish for expecting anything more.
Under the gather of snow, the dark form of the world
Reveals itself to you slowly. The future
Is an animal voice, wordless: *now* is a field
Grown strange in snowlight:
None of this has happened yet, but will.
There is a life you cannot live with, there is a night
When you will walk away, will walk
Years to come here, to stand and wait,
Reminding yourself you still believe in the abstract
Law of flesh we live our life together in,
The impossible idea of passion
That will break
You out of yourself and the cold
Impersonal body of the falling world.

THE MOON AND CONSTELLATIONS

None of the clichés will do it: *like glass: like crystal: pure*
As the driven snow. But what can you say? Branch-tips
Freeze into this air, inseparable from dusklight
As capillaries from flesh, and as incomprehensibly patterned.
Maybe that's a cliché too. It's five below zero, and due

To get colder as the sun drops. Maybe that's a fact.
In this weather, the world clarifies itself: it's a record winter,
And things are hard. All over town, cars slide
Downhill backward, spin against the way they drive.
You can hear them whine, then cough: see headlights darken

At streetside as batteries die. It's physical law
Turned ugly in the middle of Main Street. But I've driven out.
On this road nobody has traveled before me since snowfall
And the temperature's sudden plunge, I hold my own
Way steady, and watch the light take on a clarity

I'd call *luminosity* if I weren't already talking about light.
There is no word for the difference. Driving home yesterday,
I did not see how hard and separate the elm-boles jut
Out of each others' shadows, how when crows jerk into the sky,
Wary but not frightened at my passing, they seem to take

Permanent shape in the nameless color of what is not
Day and not night, but something entirely other.
That's a fact, but it may be false. There are false facts,
If a fact is a way of saying something that makes it sound true.
The fact is, the world is the same as yesterday,

Only colder, that's all, and what I want to see
As a visionary difference is only a difference in vision,
In light that makes me focus on the boundaries between things,
Their dark and believable presences in the air of almost-night.
I round a curve slowly, see the lake through a gap in the trees,

That weeks-frozen stretch of featureless dead white
I have watched every day, suspicious. Its moonscape
Is unreal to me. Once changed like that, something deep
In my body tells me, it is capable of anything. And yet
I could walk two miles across it to the other shore.

This is the physical world. Hours from now, in the dark,
I will come here again on foot, my ritual night-walk: I will stand
On the side of this road, overlook this lake,
And it will be the same road, the same lake, however half-visible:
I will come here from my cabin, with its fire and its reading light:

Will hesitate, as the white of my breath obscures what remains
To me of vision, wanting to know I am standing on the edge
Between true and false facts, between myself and the world,
Between landscape and inscape in the abstract
Moonlight, believing, not believing, come with my separate mind

And body to walk the diamond clarity of what is not
Snow and not ice but another substance partaking
Of two states of being, two names, two truths. But I'll find,
As I have always found, that when I lift my hand
Against whatever shatter of moon there is, to block that light

So the permanent pattern of stars can come to me clearly,
It is only my hand I'll look at, its five-pointed shadow
Hung there among the mythic orders, clichéd as all
The rest, and maybe no realer, but more loved
By the people I love, who, loving, hold it blindly

To the one great law of the physical,
The body, which appropriates everything.